IMAGES
of America

ENERGEN
CORPORATION

NOTE FROM THE CEO

In looking through this pictorial history, I hope you gain an appreciation for Energen's past. Reminiscent of a yearbook, this work is filled with images exemplifying who we are, what we do, where we have been, and why we have been in business for the last 150 years. It is a reminder of the challenges and the successes along the way—and the opportunities that lie ahead.

Many of the photographs selected for this book highlight employees at work and in the community. No company will be successful year after year without an enthusiastic and dedicated workforce. Energen's 1,500 employees nationwide are, without a doubt, a major factor in our continuing corporate success.

The impact of this workforce is evident in the accomplishments of the last 20 to 30 years. Some of the more notable activities, projects, or challenges include

Strategic Planning	*Y2K*	*Alabama Gas Light and Grill*
Diversification	*Burlington Acquisition*	*Transco Connection*
Regulation and Deregulation	*San Juan Basin*	*Incentive Plan*
Inventing Our Future	*First Permian Acquisition*	*TOTAL Minatome Acquisition*
100 Best Companies to Work for	*RSE*	*Customer Service Training*
in America	*23 Municipal Acquisitions*	*G.E. Pipeline*
Operation Assist	*Winter of 1976–1977*	*Winter of 2000–2001*
Alagasco Energy to Taurus	*PRIDE celebrations*	*Pipelines for electric generation*
Taurus to Energen Resources	*Mercedes - Vance*	*New Liquefier for Pinson LNG*
Coalbed methane	*Olympic Torch Run*	*Operator Certification*
Exiting offshore exploration	*EGN Services*	*Hyundai - Montgomery*
CATS		

This list is a brief reminder of our recent corporate journey. Using our aggressive strategic growth plan, we made fundamental changes, and moved away from the traditional gas utility model toward a more diversified energy company that can compete in the energy marketplace of the 21st century. And, as we move into our next strategic phase, our future appears to be just as exciting and challenging as our past.

—Wm. Michael Warren, Jr.
Chairman, President and CEO
September 2002

(Photo courtesy of Deborah Thornhill.)

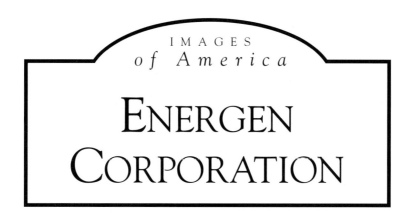

IMAGES
of America

ENERGEN
CORPORATION

The 150 Committee
Sandra Behel, editor

ARCADIA

Published by Arcadia Publishing,
an imprint of Tempus Publishing, Inc.
2 Cumberland Street
Charleston, SC 29401

Printed in Great Britain.

Library of Congress Catalog Card Number: 2002107352

For all general information contact Arcadia Publishing at:
Telephone 843-853-2070
Fax 843-853-0044
E-Mail sales@arcadiapublishing.com

For customer service and orders:
Toll-Free 1-888-313-2665

Visit us on the internet at http://www.arcadiapublishing.com

Burning eternally in Birmingham's Woodrow Wilson Park is the Flame of Freedom, honoring the Jefferson County veterans of all wars. The American Legion sponsored the dignified and impressive monument, topped by the gas flame. The photograph highlighting the dedication ceremonies shows marine staff sergeants Frank A. Hutchins and William C. Smith standing guard. The eternal flame, a fitting symbol in the form of a Flame of Freedom all-weather gas torch, commemorated the American Legion's 50th anniversary. (Courtesy of Energen Collection.)

The 150 Committee selected this photograph in memory and honor of the victims of the September 11, 2001 attacks. May the Flame of Freedom continue to burn bright in honor of all veterans and victims, police, fire department, and port authority personnel.

CONTENTS

ACKNOWLEDGMENTS

This book would not exist without a volunteer committee known as "The 150." The committee, consisting of members from the various companies, divisions, and departments, came together with a goal to develop a pictorial history of the Energen story. The committee members solicited photographs and other memorabilia from current employees and retirees. The 150 Committee members were Debbie Barber, Sandra Behel, Connie Blalock, Stephanie Cannon, Robert Clayton, Mary Cooper, Beverly Cox, Renee Davis, Susan Delanne, Paul Ferguson, Charlene Gilbert, Paige Goldman, Denise Griffin, Veria Hardy, Celeste Hartfield, Sherry Hendrix, Doug Honeycutt, Lilla Hood, Sandra Hooks, Donna Jackson, Fred Kilgore, Alfred Morris, Vera Mullinax, Ann Nelson, Jamie Nelson, Ken Nichols, Ellen Phillips, Wanda Pointer, Jennifer Smith, Aleene Taunton, Theresa Taylor, Judy Tramble, Deborah Walker, Gary Warner, Roger Weeks, Brunson White, Carolyn S. Williams, Lisa Wilson, and Gary Youngblood.

The Energen Archival Collection in the Corporate Records Department, the Communications Department's photographic library, divisions, employees, and retirees provided the photographs contained in this pictorial history. These photographs are identified as "(Courtesy of Energen Collection)." Many of the photographs first appeared in the company communication tool, *GASLINES*, or as part of the *Energen Annual Report*. If a photographer noted a request for credit on a particular photograph, then that credit is given. In some instances, the committee reused the original *GASLINES* or *Energen Annual Report* caption as part of the narrative.

In addition, the committee collected historical information to use with the photographs from a variety of sources including Charles E. Knight's manuscript "It's Been a Gasser," Rex Lysinger's Newcomen Society speech "The Energen Story," Wayne Flynt's book *Mine, Mill & Microchip*, and Catherine White's "The Story of Alabama Gas Corporation: A Contemporary Legend.".

This early mobile sales promotion for the gas industry probably attracted as much attention by sound as it did by sight. The American gas industry was born in Baltimore in 1816. (Courtesy of Energen Collection.)

In 1998, Energen Corp. moved into its new corporate headquarters. Energen renewed its commitment to maintaining the vitality of downtown Birmingham by keeping its new headquarters building in the heart of the "Magic City." (Courtesy of Energen Collection.)

INTRODUCTION

Energen Corporation traces its beginnings back to October 14, 1852, when the City Council of Montgomery passed an ordinance granting John Jeffrey and Company of Cincinnati, Ohio, a franchise to provide gas lighting to the city. The next year Jeffrey and Company sold its rights and H.H. Hilliard, Charles T. Pollard, Seth Robinson, John S. Winter, and others organized the Montgomery Gas Light Company. John Jeffrey and Company contracted to build the plant. The General Assembly of Alabama passed an act to incorporate the Montgomery Gas Light Company (MGLC) in November 1853. The incorporation act stated that the company had a subscribed capital stock of $75,000 for the extension of gas pipes and could increase up to $100,000 if necessary. The company's first product was manufactured gas produced at a Montgomery plant located on the Alabama River. MGLC's distribution system began operation on February 7, 1854, with service to Montgomery including the state capitol.

The Company continued operating throughout the Civil War; however, the coal used to produce manufactured gas became difficult to acquire. MGLC, or as the *Montgomery Advertiser* referred to them, the "gas-house-gang," improvised by generating a gas using a process of carbonizing logs. In the late 1800s, the company built a new plant and changed its name to Montgomery Light & Power Company. Mergers and name changes continued in the first part of the 1900s. In 1903, Montgomery Light and Power Company became Montgomery Light and Water Power Company. Later, Alabama Power Company purchased the Company in 1923.

After six years, Alabama Power Company sold the gas system to Alabama Utilities Service Company. Alabama Utilities, a company formed with the specific objective of acquiring gas properties in Alabama, purchased Montgomery, Anniston, Decatur, Selma, and Tuscaloosa as part of its acquisition plan. In October 1930, Montgomery converted its system from manufactured gas to natural gas.

Southern Natural Gas Company acquired Alabama Gas Company and its holdings in May 1937. Southern also acquired Alabama Natural Gas Corporation with gas systems in Auburn, Birmingham, Heflin, Huntsville, Leeds, Opelika, Reform, Tuskegee, and Wetumpka. In 1948, Southern Natural merged Alabama Gas Company and Birmingham Gas Company into Alabama Gas Corporation. The next year, the Corporation sold the two north Alabama systems, Decatur and Huntsville, to the respective municipal governments.

In 1953, Southern Natural Gas Company was ordered to divest itself of the distribution company. Alabama Gas Corporation was spun off, becoming a publicly traded independent company.

Positioning itself for the future in 1974, the Company formed Alagasco, Inc., a holding company, with Alabama Gas Corporation as its primary subsidiary. In 1985, the holding company became Energen Corporation. Today, Energen Corporation is a diversified energy company with two major subsidiaries, Alagasco, its natural gas utility, and Energen Resources, its oil and gas acquisition and production company.

Tracing the company history through the various predecessor companies, a common theme develops. Each reorganization, acquisition, or merger created an environment that required company leaders to anticipate possible opportunities or challenges to the company's continued success.

Amazingly, the Company began before the Civil War, the pony express, and the establishment of the Western Union Telegraph Company among other major events and infrastructure developments in America. The Company has a history that spans 150 years. It has survived economic recessions and depressions, civil and world wars, the cold war, the civil rights movement, and the energy crisis among other challenges.

Alabama Gas has documented its successes and challenges with photographs, especially in the latter half of the 20th century. Starting in 1948, a company newsletter and magazine, *GASLINES*, provided information on current activities within the company. These

Alabama Gas Corporation has had a presence in downtown Birmingham from the 1930s to the present. This picture depicts one of the earlier headquarters known as the "1918 building." (Courtesy of Energen Collection.)

Many things have changed since the company's beginnings in 1852. There is a vast difference in the trucks in 2002 compared to the first trucks used by the company. (Courtesy of Energen Collection.)

publications provide a glimpse of the employees and now serve as rich resource into the past. GASLINES often carried articles concerning the community activities and interests of the employees that went beyond work interests.

In this pictorial history, the chapter titles represent components of a flame to reflect the factors of Alabama Gas Corporation's progression into Energen Corporation. The components are the spark, heart, warmth, and glow of the flame. It takes a spark to get a flame to burn—this represents the vision and planning over the years to grow into Energen Corporation, which is covered in chapter one. The employees of Energen make up the heart of the flame in chapter two. With their dedication and commitment to the task at hand, they rise to the challenges before them. Community involvement or corporate citizenship is the warmth of the Energen flame in chapter three. Volunteerism abounds at Energen and its subsidiaries. Chapter four, the glow of the flame, reflects Energen's approach toward customers and stockholders. Chapter five looks toward the future. Each chapter begins with recent history and moves back in time to demonstrate the changes and consistencies of the Company over the last 150 years.

The 150 Committee enjoyed selecting the photographs and hopes the final product provides an informative glimpse at the Corporation's history. The photographs and historical notes are representative of the vast collection of talent and projects over the years. With 150 years of history, it was impossible to cover all companies, departments, and programs of Energen, Alagasco, and Energen Resources, but it is the hope of the committee that readers will enjoy this overview.

This photograph shows one of the first gas fitting trucks used by the gas company. One of the men is a former employee, Arthur Hopper, and the other is unidentified. (Courtesy of Energen Collection.)

One

THE SPARK OF THE FLAME

Every flame needs a spark. For Energen, that spark is the vision of the company's leadership. In the late 20th century and first part of the 21st century, Energen and its leaders prepared five-year strategic plans. Through this process, they identified critical issues, potential strengths, and weaknesses to determine the goals and objectives for the success of the corporation. Often, that meant change. For the first five years of the 21st century, the vision called for new technology and business initiatives. Previous visions included diversification and acquisitions. In 1953, the vision was to become a publicly traded corporation. Southern Natural Gas envisioned the merger of small utilities into one corporation in the 1930s and 1940s. And, of course, the first vision in 1852 was to light the streets of Montgomery, Alabama's state capital.

Throughout Alagasco's illustrious history, acquisitions and mergers have played a key role in the growth of the company. In October 2001, Alagasco purchased its 23rd municipal gas utility within 16 years to expand its customer base. In the above photograph, Bill Bibb, vice president of Birmingham operations (left), presents a check to Columbiana mayor Allan Lowe and city councilmen Tom Seale and Leslie Whiting. The transaction finalized the sale of Columbiana's gas system to Alagasco. (Courtesy of Energen Collection.)

Gary Youngblood became president of Alabama Gas Corporation in 1997. Youngblood's vision for Alagasco included additional pipeline construction, economic development partnerships, technology initiatives, employee pride and ownership, improved customer service, and service hero awards. In 2002, Alagasco served approximately 470,000 customers. (Courtesy of Deborah Thornhill.)

In 2002, Energen began a business initiative, known as "Inventing Our Future." The initiative's goal is to make Energen become a more efficient and more competitive company. The first two projects have the names Enterprise Resource Management Application (ERMA) and Mapping and Geographic Information (MAGI). (Courtesy of Billy Brown.)

New technologies and safety procedures protect employees and customers. Here, Alagasco employees set up a gauge to monitor the pressure on a broken main as they make the necessary repairs. (Courtesy of Energen Collection.)

13

In 1999, Alagasco and other natural gas companies across the country voluntarily began to place safety devices on residential gas lines at no cost to customers. The Excess Flow Value (EFV) is a safety device intended for use on all new and replaced single-residential services. (Courtesy of Energen Collection.)

For the first 100 years of the company's existence, men dug the pipeline trenches with picks and shovels. In the 21st century, a trencher and other large equipment reduce the amount of time and manual energy required to expand a pipeline to a new location. (Courtesy of Energen Collection.)

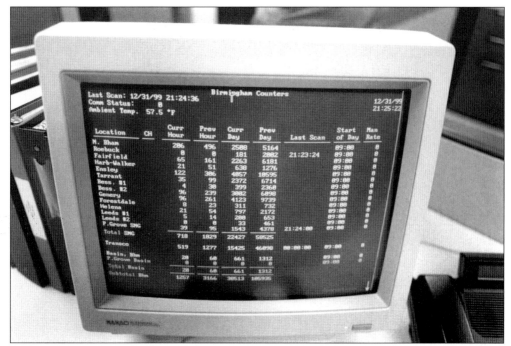

In the 1990s, corporations around the world, including Energen and its subsidiaries, developed strategic plans and special task forces to address the possible problems relating to the turn of the century, or Y2K, as it became known. (Courtesy of Energen Collection.)

Brunson White, vice president and CIO, watches local, national, and international coverage of New Year celebrations and for any problems identified as a Y2K problem for each time zone. To many people, Y2K was a non-event. However, it was a non-event only because of the hard work and planning that had resolved concerns before they could become problems. (Courtesy of Energen Collection.)

In May 2002, Alagasco quadrupled the liquifaction capacity of the Pinson LNG. When the winter heating season approaches, Alagasco's employees ensure that the company's peak-shaving facilities, such as the Pinson LNG Plant, are ready to provide peak-day gas supplies as needed. (Courtesy of Energen Collection.)

Mike Warren became president of Alagasco in 1984. All of Alagasco's presidents stressed safety as an issue for its employees, especially when driving and representing the company. For example, in 2001, Alagasco president Gary Youngblood and the Safety Department promoted safety issues through, "Have a Good Day, Alagasco." (Courtesy of Energen Corporation.)

In 1997, James McManus became president of the oil and gas exploration subsidiary, Taurus Exploration Inc., now known as Energen Resources Corporation. Energen Resources's major acquisitions to date include the purchase of San Juan Basin properties in New Mexico from Burlington Resources, coalbed methane properties in Alabama from Amoco and Burlington, TOTAL Minatome Corporation, and First Permian, among others. (Courtesy of Deborah Thornhill.)

From 1995 to 1998, Taurus acquired approximately $345 million of producing oil and gas properties, spent $45 million developing these properties, and invested another $65 million to explore for and develop new reservoirs. Taurus also has expanded geographically, establishing bases of operation in the San Juan Basin in New Mexico and the Permian Basin in West Texas. In July 1998, the Energen board of directors announced a name change for Taurus Exploration Inc. It was important to change to a name that more closely identified itself with the holding company. Taurus Exploration Inc. became Energen Resources Corporation. (Above courtesy of Energen Collection; below courtesy of Billy Brown.)

This San Juan Basin drilling rig is a reflection of the rapidly growing oil and gas business through which Energen Resources can focus on the acquisition of producing oil and gas properties with varying levels of development potential. (Courtesy of Billy Brown.)

After the company finds natural gas or oil reserves, the next step is to get the product to market. This may require gas pipeline construction. (Courtesy of Energen Collection.)

Energen has an outstanding reputation for ethical behavior and fair dealing that has been earned over many years. This reputation has been achieved through adherence to Energen's Statement of Principles. These principles are the foundation of a standard of conduct expected of every Energen employee—in every business relationship—at all times. However, it is sometimes difficult to be certain of the right course of conduct. Energen established business conduct guidelines and appointed a corporate compliance officer to provide guidance in making the right decisions. Dudley C. Reynolds serves as Energen's general counsel, secretary, and corporate compliance officer. (Courtesy of Energen Collection.)

Following the Y2K project, management identified the need for a long-range technology vision. Geoff C. Ketcham, executive vice president and chief financial officer, serves as chairman of the Information Technology Initiative Council. The new vision led to the establishment of a Project Management Office in 2000 and a five-year plan. Energen launched "Inventing Our Future," its newest technology and business initiative plan, in 2001–2002. (Courtesy of Deborah Thornhill.)

20

Mike Warren became president of Alabama Gas Corporation in 1984. During his tenure, Alagasco experienced construction growth with the building of three major pipelines connecting to a less expensive interstate supply of gas, the purchase of 23 municipal systems, and Alagasco being named in *The 100 Best Companies To Work For In America* by Robert Levering and Milton Moskowitz (also listed in *Fortune* magazine). He launched the "We Take Pride" program. PRIDE stands for being "performance-oriented, willing to take risks, innovative, determined, and enthusiastic." The *Birmingham News/Post Herald* selected Warren as "CEO of the Year" in 2001. (Courtesy of Energen Collection.)

The leadership styles of Mike Warren and Rex Lysinger emphasized strategic planning, business ethics, and community involvement. Their management teams developed plans and objectives to position Energen for the 21st century and to develop a workforce with skill sets to meet that challenge. The initial steps into diversification required purchasing or developing partnerships with other companies to find the appropriate match for the solidly performing public utility. (Courtesy of Billy Brown.)

In February 1989, Energen purchased W&J Propane Co. Inc. The purchase meant even further diversification of the company's line of business. Propane offered strong competition in all-electric rural areas. (Courtesy of Energen Collection.)

Taurus was a national leader in the development of coalbed methane as a supply source. Today, coalbed methane accounts for nine percent of the nation's natural gas reserves. (Courtesy of Energen Collection.)

Energen Resources significantly expanded its Permian Basin operations with the First Permian acquisition, which was finalized on April 8, 2002. The acquisition resulted in an additional estimated 43 million barrels of oil equivalent reserves in the Permian Basin in west Texas. The purchase price was $120 million in cash and 3,043,479 shares of Energen common stock valued at $23.95 per share. The acquisition added over 500 producing wells and nearly 350 injection wells to the Midland operations. (Courtesy of Energen Collection.)

This pumpjack on a coalbed methane well in Alabama pumped water from coal zones. This process keeps the water off the coal zones and the natural gas flows into the wellbore. (Courtesy of Energen Collection.)

As president of Alabama Gas Corporation, Warren introduced a new program entitled Alabama Gas Corporation University (AGCU), which provided employees an in-depth look at the company. After learning about all aspects of the company's operations, participants work in different teams to address a case study. A highlight of the program is the CEO chat. When the program concludes, employees leave with a new perspective on their individual roles in accomplishing the company's goals and objectives. The three-day program is held twice a year at the 4-H Conference Center. Participants are selected from employees nominated by their department heads, division managers, or functional officers. (Courtesy of Energen Collection.)

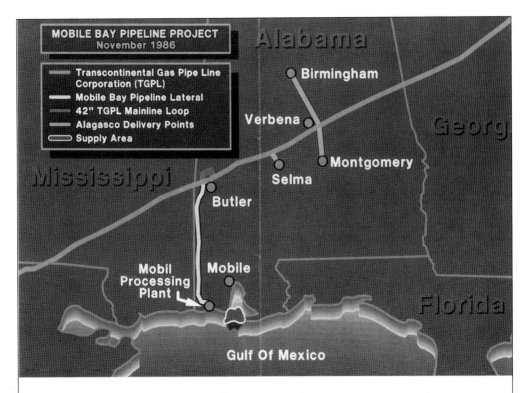

The Mobile Bay Natural Gas Project

The Mobile Bay Natural Gas Project is a combined effort among three leading U.S. energy companies to produce, market and transport natural gas from Mobile Bay, Alabama. Together, subsidiaries of Energen Corporation, Transco Energy Company and Mobil Oil Corporation will unlock the rich natural gas reserves found in Alabama's coastal waters.

The Mobile Bay Pipeline, a new 123-mile pipeline, will be built as part of the project, with capacity to deliver 250 million cubic feet per day (MMcf/d) of Mobile Bay natural gas reserves in the state of Alabama. Once future compression is added, system capacity will increase to 930 MMcf/d. Construction of the $66 million project is scheduled to begin in March of 1987 and initial gas volumes are expected to begin flowing by October 1987.

Alabama Gas, in a joint news conference with two other energy companies, made front-page headlines in newspapers across the state in November 1986 by announcing a joint venture for producing, marketing, and transporting natural gas from Mobile Bay. The other two companies involved in the project were Mobil Oil Exploration and Producing Southeast, Inc. and Transco Energy Co. Basin Pipeline Corporation, another Energen subsidiary in 1986; Transco jointly constructed the pipeline. Alagasco signed a 15-year contract with Transco Energy Marketing Co. to buy gas produced by Mobil Oil Exploration and Producing Southeast, Inc. The purchase of the Mobile Bay gas provided a firm, competitively priced gas supply for Alagasco customers into the 21st century. (Courtesy of Energen Collection.)

Rex J. Lysinger was elected president of Alabama Gas in 1977. In 1979, the company reorganized into a holding company, Alagasco, Inc., and Alabama Gas Corporation was its primary subsidiary. The oil and gas exploration company, at that time called Alagasco Energy Co., was the other subsidiary. The formation of the holding company separated the regulated utility activities from its non-utility activities. In 1981, Rex was elected president and CEO of the holding company, Alagasco, Inc. and in 1982, the title of chairman was added. In October 1985, the name of the holding company was changed to Energen Corporation in order to reflect the company's diversified business activities. At the same time, the oil and gas subsidiary became Taurus Exploration Corporation. Today, Energen is a diversified energy holding company listed on the New York Stock Exchange. Lysinger brought a vision of a diversified energy company, a reliance on strategic planning, and an abiding commitment to ethical business practices. (Courtesy of Billy Brown.)

Using Lysinger's plan for diversification, Alagasco conducted an aggressive municipal acquisition program and Taurus Exploration expanded in the oil and gas production area. Energen added Basin, Graves, American Heat Tech, and W&J Propane as subsidiaries. Taurus identified its specific niche in coalbed methane production, and Energen divested itself of Graves, American Heat Tech, and W&J Propane. In addition, subsidiaries and employees investigated ways to improve work productivity and customer services. Change and innovation are words that describe the Lysinger years of service. (Courtesy of Energen Collection.)

As CEO of Energen and President of Birmingham Chamber of Commerce, Lysinger participated in the Olympic Torch Run in 1984. The run promoted youth development programs. In addition to the run, Lysinger lit the "Olympic Torch" displayed throughout the city of Birmingham. Alagasco employees designed and built the special torch. Their ingenuity allowed the "Olympic Torch" to travel to different locations on the back of a trailer. (Courtesy of Energen Collection.)

In its early years, Taurus partnered with others in offshore drilling efforts. Energen Resources exited the offshore market to concentrate on a lower risk strategy of acquisition and exploitation of on-shore producing properties. (Courtesy of Billy Brown.)

Richard A. Puryear (right) made many contributions to his industry, to service and civic organizations, and to his government at all levels—local, state, and national. In 1930, he started with Alabama Utilities as a meter reader in Selma. He served as president of Alabama Gas Corporation from 1956 to 1973. Howard Higgins believed that the keys to success in the 1970s lay in a highly skilled, more flexible, and more productive workforce, and adoption of new techniques and ideas, as well as expansion of the marketing program. Mr. Higgins (left) served as president from 1973 to 1977 and continued to serve as CEO of Alagasco, Inc. until 1982. (Courtesy of Energen Collection.)

As part of Alagasco's program to update its feeder mains, one of the two main sources of gas serving the City of Montgomery underwent major improvements. A 12-inch feeder main, 1,500 feet in length replaced two 6-inch mains formerly in use. The main, completed in September 1971, was of heavy wall steel pipe weighted and shielded with a two-inch jacket of concrete. Seven hundred feet of its length lies buried in the bed of the Alabama River as it crosses the river near Coosada. (Courtesy of Energen Collection.)

As is the case with most river crossing construction, one of the principal problems encountered was obtaining a usable trench in the riverbed. Alagasco employed professional divers, supplied by a Mobile firm, to execute all underwater inspections. The inspections included testing for proper depth and removal of obstructions, as well as verifying that all pipes was properly covered with fill at the project's completion. (Courtesy of Energen Collection.)

In August 1957, Richard A. Puryear Jr. announced plans for construction of a gas production plant in Montgomery, Alabama. The plant was designed to store and process propane gas for ultimate blending with natural gas. The planned plant capacity was 300,000 cubic feet per hour of 1350 BTU blended gas so that the plant could operate more than five days continuously without replenishment of the propane supply. Using the most modern engineering techniques and building materials, Alagasco was a pioneer company in the south for storing gas in its liquefied state. (Courtesy of Energen Collection.)

Alagasco's liquefied natural gas (LNG) storage tanks were designed and constructed to meet all federal and state safety requirements. The facilities have been properly maintained and modernized through the years to assure maximum public protection. Alagasco LNG plants are manned around the clock by specially trained personnel. The corporation began the replacement the Pinson LNG location liquefier in 2001. The new construction included a new control room with a computer-driven distribution control system. (Courtesy of Billy Brown.)

After several years of service, the company retired the Montgomery Propane Plant in 1984. With the introduction and use of Liquefied Natural Gas (LNG) plants, the propane plants were not as cost effective. (Courtesy of Energen Collection.)

In April 1964, Richard A. Puryear, Jr., president, announced the beginning of the Liquefied Natural Gas (LNG) plant to be located in Pinson, Alabama. Alagasco was one of the first gas distribution companies in the United States utilizing advanced technology for construction of facilities for liquefaction, storage, and vaporization of natural gas. (Courtesy of Energen Collection.)

Hugh Reid Derrick became president of Alagasco in April 1953. During his administration, the company installed new communication technologies including a radio dispatch system, WBXI. A community-minded leader, Derrick established Junior Achievement groups at all Alagasco locations throughout the state. Before his presidency, he worked as a superintendent in Tuscaloosa, a manager in Gadsden and Montgomery, and was vice president of operations. After Derrick left the company in 1956, Richard A. Puryear Jr. served as president. Joe N. Greene continued his service as chairman of the board. (Courtesy of Energen Collection.)

Pictured from left to right are Terry Brannon, Sue Parsons, Jackie Baldwin, Elvis Walton (advisor), Frances Petrazeulla, Gordon Johnston (advisor), Frank Tarrant, Calvin Yother (advisor), Vincent Manella, Julian Morris (advisor), and Alice England. The 1954 Junior Achievement group was the first such group for Alabama Gas. Junior Achievement programs teach young people between the ages 15 and 21 the methods of conducting business under the free-enterprise system. (Courtesy of Charlie Preston Studios.)

Alagasco installed mobile radios in service vehicles in 1941, the first in the nation for a gas distribution company. (Courtesy of Energen Collection.)

Joseph N. Greene was Alagasco's first president. It was during his tenure as president and chairman that Alabama Gas Corp. attained much of its initial growth. There were 175,000 customers and earnings were $1.3 million when Alabama Gas became a publicly traded company in 1953. Customers increased to 240,000 and earnings increased to $1.7 million under his leadership. He was an energetic civic leader for nearly 30 years. Greene was in the forefront of most efforts to make Birmingham a better and healthier community. He was a member of the Birmingham 100—an organization designed to bring industry to Birmingham. In 1953, he was elected "Birmingham Man of the Year." Greene wanted a way to communicate with all employees to keep them informed of the company's activities and plans. This desire led to the development of GASLINES, the company's monthly magazine. (Courtesy of Energen Collection.)

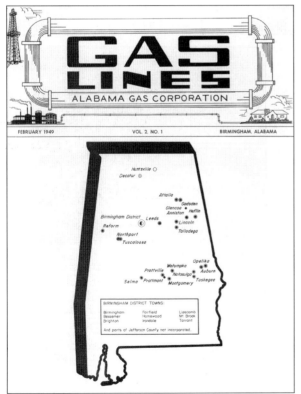

The merger of Alabama Gas with Birmingham Gas was completed on December 27, 1948 and the company operated under its new name Alabama Gas Corp. The February 1949 GASLINES provided a map that showed the various cities and towns in which the new company operated. (Courtesy of Energen Collection.)

An Opelika Division employee used this car on his route in Auburn to read meters. The story is told that one day while he read meters at Auburn University, a group of the football players picked up the car and put it on the top of the stairs of a university building. Rather than making a scene, the meter reader got in his car and drove it down the stairs. (Courtesy of Energen Collection.)

One Hundred Fifty Years

Montgomery	1852
Selma	1854
Birmingham	1879
Anniston	1887
Gadsden	1887
Tuscaloosa	1900
Opelika/Auburn	1930
Energen Resources	1971

Two
THE HEART OF
THE FLAME

Employees make up the heart of the flame and are a major factor in the success of Energen and its subsidiaries, Alagasco and Energen Resources. They take the strategic vision or spark of the flame and identify their role in how to make the vision a reality. The slogan "We Take Pride and Ownership" aptly fits the work environment at Energen. Employees take pride in their work, their company, and their communities. And, their dedication to the challenge at hand often is the reason for a project's success.

Employees promoted their company pride and Alagasco was listed as one the "100 Best Companies to Work for in America" in 1992, 1998, and 1999.(Courtesy of Energen Collection.)

Pride comes in many forms, and as these employees point out, it can even come gift-wrapped. Employees from across the state put on their Santa hats and climbed in a gift box to show their company pride. (Courtesy of Geoff Knight.)

As evidenced in some of the photographs included in this book, the employee base reflected the times and culture. The company has changed in a variety of ways including employment practices and management styles. For example, in the 1990s, the company leadership started an initiative to enhance the working relations of its diverse employee base. The company began diversity training and created a diversity council in each area. The Community Affairs Committee (CAC) of Operation New Birmingham presented a Liberty and Justice Award to Alagasco during its September 1998 meeting. Alagasco received an award in the business category. Alagasco was recognized for its efforts to enhance race relations in the community and for its corporate diversity programs. (Courtesy of Energen Collection.)

One area of consistency for the company is the company tradition of emphasis on community involvement. The company's involvement in the annual United Way campaigns continued to increase. Employees have always answered the United Way appeal with open hearts and generous giving. These Selma employees toured several United Way agencies as part of their 1999 campaign. (Courtesy of Energen Collection.)

Employees were at the core of the success of the Y2K preparedness project. On New Year's Eve 1999, employees knew their role to assure that Energen was prepared for all contingencies. Employees had a late-night supper—after midnight—once it was evident that no technical glitches had occurred. (Courtesy of Energen Collection.)

Birmingham Division employees received the first "Alagasco Presidential Helping Hands Award" in June 1998. It was presented at the Western Operations Center for the efforts of employees during the April tornado. Youngblood stated that he was proud of the company and its employees because when a crisis hits, everyone pulls together. (Courtesy of Energen Collection.)

The tornado that occurred in Jefferson County on April 8, 1998 touched off a whirlwind of activity for four Alagasco crews and more than 15 service mechanics that lasted throughout the night and into the next day. Whenever a disaster hits in any of the company's locations, employees immediately answer the call. (Courtesy of Energen Collection.)

Alagasco work crews walked the streets, listening for the rush of escaping gas and capping broken lines when found. (Courtesy of Energen Collection.)

There is graphic proof of the dependability of natural gas services of Alagasco. Ice storms, snowstorms, tornadoes, floods, and extreme cold weather are just a few weather events the company has endured. Customers of Alagasco know what dependability of natural gas service means to them. (Courtesy of Energen Collection.)

This fountain located at Court Square in downtown Montgomery was frozen solid during an ice storm in the winter of 1977. Alagasco employees maintained quality service and gas supply throughout the storm. (Courtesy of Energen Collection.)

An ice storm in Gadsden left a frigid stillness to everything except the warm, friendly glow of the picturesque gaslight. (Courtesy of Energen Collection.)

Energen employees have a variety of job responsibilities throughout the company. From field operations to public relations, every employee has an important role in the success and future of the company. (Courtesy of Energen Collection.)

Employees participate on special projects or committees. These four employees volunteered to help on the pictorial history and became part of the group known as the "150 Committee." Pictured from left to right are Doug Honeycutt, Fred Kilgore, Donna Jackson, and Wanda Pointer. (Courtesy of Energen Collection.)

Garden shows are one of the many promotional tools used to reach potential new customers and longtime customers. Here, Talladega employees represent Alagasco at a local garden show. (Courtesy of Energen Collection.)

Computer technology changed the way many employees do their jobs over the years. Energen Resources employees now use computers to help identify and evaluate potential production areas. (Courtesy of Energen Collection.)

Energen Resources and Alagasco engineers use computers for mapping their sites. With technology advances, the number of maps stored in the offices declined. However, paper maps and drawings remain a part of the day-to-day operations for both companies. Pictured here from left to right are Greg Jennings and Robert Fleenor of Energen Resources. (Courtesy of Billy Brown.)

In the 1980s, Energen formed various companies as part of the strategic plan to diversify the corporation. These companies added a number of new faces and job positions to the overall employee base. Graves Well Drilling Co., Basin Corp., and Magnolia Pipeline were just three of the companies that changed the employee makeup. (Courtesy of Billy Brown.)

In 1991, Taurus employees Mike Findley and Kathy Plant monitored the quality of water produced during coalbed methane development as it is aerated before discharge. (Courtesy of Energen Collection.)

Graves Well Drilling Co. provided a full line of water well services for almost 40 years. Graves expanded its activities into coalbed degasification and included conventional oil and gas well drilling. The employees were known for their professionalism and expertise in their fields. (Courtesy of Energen Collection.)

The Montgomery office staff designed and wore new gold pants suits, skirt and tunic duos, and dresses of the same color, which they adopted as their office uniform for 1971. The women, in keeping with current fashion trends, selected these outfits and they wore them each Monday and Friday. The women purchased the material and made the garments themselves. They added brown stitching to provide a note of contrast to the gold material. All agreed they had as much fun making the designs of their choice as they did wearing them. (Courtesy of Energen Collection.)

In the 1950s and 1960s, 90 percent of the Home Service Department's work occurred outside the office. The backbone of Home Service was "Home Call." Staff members made calls to all customers that bought gas appliances. The Home Economist traveled to the customer's home to provide information on the use and care of the new appliance and recipes. Probably, the best known of all Home Service activities was the cooking demonstration. Office and Home Service Department staff often wore identical outfits. (Courtesy of Horace Perry.)

The Home Service Department participated in the "Old Stove Round-up" promotional events each year. They wore western attire for their cooking demonstrations and in the office during "Round-up" days. (Courtesy of Energen Collection.)

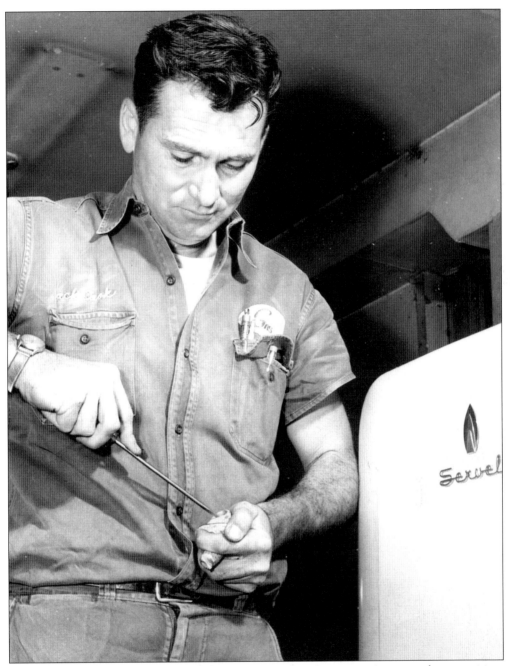

In 1952, Alabama Gas Corp. won the American Gas Association's national competition, Division II for selling Servel Refrigerators. The Anniston *GASLINES* reporter noted in a different article that Alagasco repairmen often helped sell refrigerators to customers. Here, Jack Cook of the Montgomery Division worked on a Servel gas refrigerator. (Courtesy of Energen Collection.)

Throughout Alagasco's history, construction employees spend their time installing service lines or "miles of main." Richard Sheley, assistant chief engineer, and Tom Raines, project engineer, check construction progress on the Reece City gas line installation. (Courtesy of Energen Collection.)

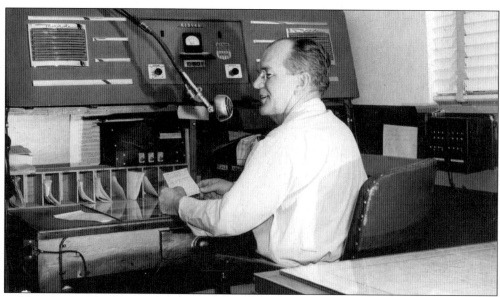

Robert Crysel, a dispatcher-clerk at the Montgomery Service Center, used the radio to contact servicemen about their next service call. Communication tools assisted employees to respond to immediate needs of various customers and locations. (Courtesy of Energen Collection.)

Alabama Gas converted from a manufactured gas to a natural gas system. This task required numerous conversion crews and was accomplished over several years. Without dedicated employees and a vision for the future, the company would not have been able to compete in the energy market in later years. This Birmingham crew was part of the conversion project. (Courtesy of Energen Collection.)

A major project in July 1955 was the conversion of a Detrex degreasing machine at Southern States Iron Roofing Co. Crewmembers, from left to right, are James Jackson, Charles Eddings, B.V. Belcher, Bob Fowler, C.R. Bowman and J.H. Patterson. (Courtesy of Charlie Preston Studios.)

Customer service representatives and office employees communicate daily with the public. Communication tools have changed over the years. From the early switchboard phone system to the interactive voice response system (IVR) and email communications, employees use technology to increase the number of customers served on a daily basis. Montgomery and Birmingham divisions have IVR in place. (Courtesy of Kealen Rice.)

One very important issue for all employees is safety. The company tracked safety records and honored successful crews or locations with awards. Ervin B. Pettit, Roy D. Wells, and their crews finished two accident-free years in 1952. From left to right are (first row) Erwin B. Pettit, Roy D. Wells, Tommy Harris, Walter Washington, Booker T. Culver, and Robert Moore; (second row) Richard Showers, Leroy Hardy, and Walter Riles; (third row) Lewis Evans, Willie Tate, John L. Pope, Robert L. Operton, Willie T. Henry, and Willie Hampton. (Courtesy of Kealen Rice.)

Employees like these from Opelika proudly served their different divisions and districts. Before the conversion to natural gas, Alagasco distributed coke-oven gas in some areas and manufactured gas in others. Both of these gases are primarily produced through a process of burning coal. (Courtesy of Charles Jernigan.)

Montgomery installation and maintenance crewmen readied the truck for their daily work in the 1940s. (Courtesy of Collier & Kraus.)

The meter readers recorded their readings in ledger books. Here, Leonard Cox is shown reading a Montgomery customer's meter. (Courtesy of Energen Collection.)

Labor unions always have been a part of Alagasco's history. AFL Gasfitters Local 548 is Alagasco's oldest bargaining unit. The union's members are construction, service, and distribution mechanics and apprentices, as well as meter readers and utility men, who work outside the Birmingham Division. In addition to the 548, other union locals within Alagasco include USWA locals 12030 and 12030A. All of the union locals negotiate contracts as necessary. (Courtesy of Billy Brown.)

The softball team provided an excellent opportunity for fellow employees to get to know each other outside the work environment. (Courtesy of Energen Collection.)

The Alagasco Flames women's softball teams enjoyed their time together and showed their company pride and spirit on the field. In 1981, the team was very successful in the summer tournaments. (Courtesy of Energen Collection.)

Employees showed company pride by organizing a bowling team and competing with other community businesses for the bowling title in their area. It was a good way to have fun and keep the company name in front of the public. The Montgomery team members, from left to right, are (front) George Sims and Ray Graham; (back) Larry Overman, Larry Bryson, Stanley Slater, and Sam Harris. (Courtesy of Energen Collection.)

Company softball and baseball teams were common in the 1940s and 1950s. Before the Civil Rights Movement, teams were separated by race. By the 1970s, the teams integrated and women developed company teams. From left to right are (kneeling) Paul Patrick, Dadie McRight, Charles Owsley, Cleveland Ross, and Paul Sansom; (standing) Joe Torrillo, Ernest Evans, Ralph Gillespie, Tom Cowart, and Dalton Shaw. This is one of the Montgomery teams from 1949. (Courtesy of Energen Collection.)

This is one of the Birmingham teams from 1948. From left to right are Harry Martin, John Posey, John Findley, Richard Hardon, Tommie Jones, Will Austin, Will Sheppard, Elijah Chatham, James Austin, Henry Thomas, Henry Cooper, and John Hayes. (Courtesy of Energen Collection.)

This is a view of the control center at the North Birmingham pumping station built in 1958. Modern lighting, air conditioning, and soundproofing were incorporated into the design. Each of the charts, easily visible to the operator, represented one control or telemetering point along the gas mains. The control panel, at which operator L.C. Harrison is seated, contained the electronic switches that permit operation of each control valve or regulator from this central point. Looking over the control panel are, from left to right, E.W. (Winnie) Smith (chief radio engineer), and T.G. (Tommy) Humphreys Jr. (assistant chief engineering, general office). (Courtesy of Charlie Preston Studios.)

Each Alagasco service center had a warehouse. Montgomery employee Emmett Hooks logged in information relating to the inventory on a daily basis. (Courtesy of Energen Collection.)

This is a general view of the Birmingham Division's very modern new shop in 1949. The new meter shop was designed to take care of a peak load of approximately 40,000 meters per year. With a 1999 renovation project at the Birmingham Service Center, the meter shop changed to a spacious work area complete with private offices and conference rooms. From left to right, the men are G.M. Kiker Jr., M.B. McAllister, T.A. Boles, M.F. McDanal, H.A. Baker Jr., G.W. Gilmore, L.A. Tate, M.H. Lutz, E.J. Wright Jr., and W.O. Godwin. (Courtesy of Energen Collection.)

In 1949, Birmingham Division's new meter shop included the central repair room and two power rooms where incoming and outgoing meters were tested. Other rooms included a paint room, storeroom, and a separate workshop for the repair of gauges and other apparatuses. (Courtesy of Energen Collection.)

All divisions had a meter shop. This is the Montgomery meter shop in the 1920s. Pictured from left to right are Leonard H. Cox, Grant Lamar, and Edward B. Adams. (Courtesy of Energen Collection.)

Employees also assisted in technology initiatives. The Information Technology Department received a Presidential Award to celebrate Energen's successful transition into the year 2000. Alagasco president Gary Youngblood instituted this award for exceptional performance of duty. At the same time, Ferrell Maughn, Y2K director, received a service award. (Courtesy of Energen Collection.)

In 1962, Alabama Gas began preparations for the installation of an IBM 1401-16K tape system for customer billing and related applications. This system was installed in 1964. The company added additional applications such as payroll, industrial billing, meter inventory, and distribution accounting. Four years later, the company planned to upgrade to an IBM 360-40 system with 128K. With the rapid growth in computer technology, the importance of a sound technology plan grew and remained a high priority in the early years of the 21st century. (Courtesy of Energen Collection.)

From the 1940s on, Alagasco had safety programs and award mechanisms to encourage employees to maintain the highest safety levels at all times. Tuskegee employees received commendation for 317,779 man-hours without an accident to earn National Safety Council award. (Courtesy of Polks Studio.)

In February 1953, Herman Presley and crew complete their third consecutive accident-free year. The men pictured are, from left to right, (first row) Herman Presley, Eddie Perry, and Jim Miller; (second row) James I. Franks, Emmett Banks, Carvin Williams, and John Hondon. The crew worked in the Birmingham Main and Service Department. (Courtesy of Kealen Rice.)

In May 1963, Selma established a new safety record. The more than 40 Selma District employees held a record for 564,226 accident-free hours on the job. The group had not had an accident in over seven years. (Courtesy of Energen Collection.)

In 1955, The Birmingham First Avenue employees received a safety award for 500,000 man-hours for no-lost-time accidents from January 12, 1953 through June 30, 1955. (Courtesy of Charlie Preston Studios.)

The company also developed a program to honor employees for their length of service. From left to right, Opelika manager H.H. Higgins presents 25-year service awards to Frank Edwards and Samuel Brady, a 15-year award to Bill Hatter, and 10-year award to Harry Nicholas. (Courtesy of Yutmeyer's Photography.)

Alabama Gas Employees used trucks to distribute meters to new customers and replace meters in need of repair. As the company grew with acquisitions, the number of trucks seen around the state increased. (Courtesy of Stanley Paulger.)

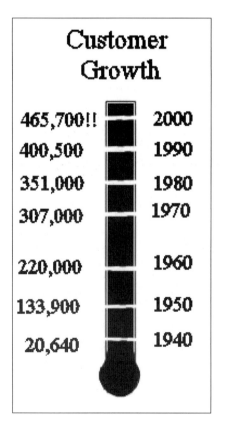

Customer Growth

465,700!!	2000
400,500	1990
351,000	1980
307,000	1970
220,000	1960
133,900	1950
20,640	1940

MUNICIPAL MULTIPLICATION

1850s	Montgomery, Selma
1880s	Birmingham, Gadsden, Anniston
1900s	Tuscaloosa, West End
1910s	Corey, East Lake, Wylam, Pratt City, North Birmingham, Woodlawn, Bessemer
1920s	Boyles, Tarrant City, Inglenook, Brighton, Hollywood, Homewood, Irondale, Lipscomb
1930s	Auburn, Opelika, Heflin, Leeds, Reform, Huntsville
1940s	Northport, Lincoln, Prattville, Prattmont, Glencoe, Blue Mountain
1950s	Holt, Brent, Centreville, Newbern, Uniontown, Marion, Shamut, Langdale, Fairfax, Weaver, Riverview, Eady City
1960s	Clay, Odenville, Springville, Branchville, Riverside, Reese City
1970s	Demopolis, Rainbow City
1980s	Steele, Alexandria, Vincent, Hale, Greene County, Phenix City, Montevallo, Hokes Bluff, Clanton, Parrish, Pell City, Eclectic, Jasper, Ashville, Oakman, Pleasant Grove, Thomaston, Double Springs, East Lauderdale
1990s	Linden, Chilton County, Alabaster, Ragland, LaFayette, Helena
2000s	Columbiana

Three

THE WARMTH OF THE FLAME

Employees and officers alike participate in outside community activities. From the 1940s to the 21st century, all of the presidents and CEOs encouraged civic involvement and the importance of corporate citizenship. This is the warmth of the flame—giving back to the community. Each location has a United Way campaign each year to encourage employees to consider giving back to the community where they live. Other organizations such as Christmas in April, Salvation Army Angel Tree, and local adopt-a-school programs are just some of the many projects employees take as their personal project for the year. In February 2000, Energen was listed among the "100 Best Corporate Citizens" by Business Ethics magazine. The list reveals the public companies that best serve stockholders, employees, customers, and communities. Energen was listed as number 83 on the list of 100.

Energen employees enjoy spending time together outside the work environment. In addition to working together in charity events, employees look forward to the annual golf tournament. The 47th annual tournament was held in Gadsden. (Courtesy of Energen Collection.)

In 2000, Gary Youngblood served as the chairman of the Central Alabama United Way Campaign Drive. (Courtesy of Energen Collection.)

Youngblood, as the Central Alabama United Way Campaign chairman, participated in various community activities to promote giving to United Way including sporting events, leadership breakfasts, and talent shows. He participated in previous campaigns including the "Slam Dunk" United Way campaign. (Courtesy of Energen Collection.)

In two consecutive pacesetter campaigns in 2000 and 2001, employees increased their giving to United Way of Central Alabama by 45 percent. In addition to the employee pledges, the corporation increased its contribution by 27 percent over the two campaigns. (Courtesy of Energen Collection.)

Each Energen location participates in a local United Way campaign. Kitty Kynard and Bob Armstrong (Selma division) chaired their local campaign. (Courtesy of Energen Collection.)

Because of the outstanding contribution to United Way from the Gadsden District, United Way recognized Alagasco by picketing in front of the commercial office. United Way picketed all businesses that were top contributors. (Courtesy of Energen Collection.)

Christmas in April is another corporate citizen event that has become an annual event. Employees from Energen, Energen Resources, and Alagasco participated in the National Rebuilders Day to renovate low-income homes in 2001. (Courtesy of Energen Collection.)

Decorator Showcases and Holiday Homes benefit Christmas in April in areas such as Tuscaloosa and Montgomery. Christmas in April is a national non-profit organization that repairs and rehabilitates the homes of low-income homeowners, particularly the homes of the elderly and disabled. (Courtesy of Energen Collection.)

Christmas in April in Lee County held its Volunteer Day on April 18, 1998. Approximately 24 employees from the Opelika Division helped make repairs to a home selected by Christmas in April staff members. (Courtesy of Energen Collection.)

Anniston March of Dimes volunteers exceeded their goal of $2,000, raising almost $2,500 during the 2001 "Walk America" campaign. The Alagasco team was awarded first place for "Most Money," a blue ribbon and first place for "T-shirt Design," and first place for "Most Participation." In addition, Alagasco and Alabama Power both were awarded first place for "Clever Container," the technique used to deliver donations. Anniston walkers were Michael Miles, Jenny Whitman, Demorra Watts, Kathy Price, Patricia Jeffrey, Tim Rider, Dylan Rider, Michael Cobb, Steve Hartley, Curtis Simpson, Sharron Crow, Angel Smith, Emily Smith, Donna Jackson, Dwight Smith, Eddie Whitman, Phillip Nunn, Lena Knighton, and Ross Knighton. (Courtesy of Energen Collection.)

Selma division employees were very involved in the 1998 March of Dimes. They held a yard sale and participated in the walk. The Walk America campaign in Selma raised $2,149. They are pictured here in front of Selma's "Flame of Freedom." (Courtesy of Energen Collection.)

In October 1999, employees from the various Birmingham locations participated in the Relay for Life to raise money for the American Cancer Society. This relay and others like it have been traditions among employees for many years. Raising almost $13,000, the 20 "Blue Flame Throwers" proved that strength is not necessarily in numbers. Strength is in caring and dedication. (Courtesy of Energen Collection.)

Employees from the Montgomery commercial office represented Alagasco at the annual March of Dimes Walk America program in 1987. (Courtesy of Energen Collection.)

Each year, Energen employees participate in the American Heart Association Jail Bail. Energen Resources employee Ann Nelson and Alagasco employee Kristi Doughty were two of the individuals listed for arrest in the 2000 drive. (Courtesy of Energen Collection.)

President and CEO Rex Lysinger was active in community affairs throughout his service at Energen. He served as chairman of the Birmingham area Chamber of Commerce, president of the American Heart Association, chairman of the Festival of Arts Salute to Germany, chairman of the Salvation Army, and chairman of the United Way of Central Alabama, among many other charitable and civic events. In the 1990s, Lysinger received the Arthritis Foundation Award, the Brotherhood Community Service Award, and the Salvation Army "Others" Award. (Courtesy of Energen Collection.)

In 2000, Energen Resources' employees hosted more than 20 honor students from Jess Lanier High School at the Vance Field Office. (Courtesy of Energen Collection.)

Energen was a platinum sponsor of the 2002 Mud Bowl 21, an Ultimate Frisbee Tournament. This annual event raised more than $40,000 for Bread and Roses, a United Way agency that provides shelter for homeless women and children. Decked out in tie-dyed T-shirts, the Energen team won two out of four games and was edged out from playing in the semi-finals. From left to right are (front row) Lilla Hood, Monica Bojo, Barry Moman, Andrew Benson, Karl Peterson, and Stephen Bartlett; (back row) Robert Fleenor, Chris Smith, David Fleenor, Amy Stuedeman, Dennis Otts, Amy Benson, Josh Moman, Mike Smitherman, Jody Seal, Dean Otts, and Suzy Farris. (Courtesy of Energen Collection.)

Energen employees have been strong supporters of the Salvation Army Angel Tree program for several years, making a joyful Christmas possible for many deserving children. (Courtesy of Energen Collection.)

Information Technology employees assembled and packed many of the toys purchased for the Salvation Army Angel Tree Program in 2000. (Courtesy of Energen Collection.)

In 2001, Energen employees expanded their Salvation Army Angel Tree Program to include forgotten angels. All of the items surrounding the tree were for forgotten angels. (Courtesy of Energen Collection.)

In Gadsden, employees wrapped presents for a local family so they would have a very special holiday season. (Courtesy of Energen Collection.)

In 1999 Energen created a "Get-A-Life" workshop. The program was designed to assist teens and their parents with preparation for college and a career. (Courtesy of Energen Collection.)

Supporting education in the various communities is one way that Energen, Alagasco, and Energen Resources demonstrated a commitment for the long term. Energen developed partnerships with local schools and school boards with its Adopt-a-School programs. Providing computers for a school computer lab is one way to invest in the children—a community's future. (Courtesy of Energen Collection.)

The Selma Division participated in the Partners in Education. Thomas Ferguson of Alagasco is shown here with students from Meadowview. (Courtesy of Energen Collection.)

Burnie, "the Blue Flame," makes a special appearance at one of the company's adopt-a-school locations. In an effort to communicate "The Story of Natural Gas" program with younger children more effectively, the consumer and community affairs department created Burnie. (Courtesy of Energen Collection.)

Alagasco employees of Tuscaloosa Division attend a pride celebration for their adopt-a-school at University Place. (Courtesy of Energen Collection.)

Tuscaloosa students at University Place School have their own PRIDE program. Each month a student is selected as the best representative of the PRIDE acronym—Positive, Respectful, Independent, Dependable, and Eager to learn. (Courtesy of Energen Collection.)

Taurus selected Brookwood High School as one of their community projects. (Courtesy of Energen Collection.)

Once again, Energen Special People validated the acronym (ESP) working with some very special people. On May 7, 2001, Energen employees volunteered their time to help children with special needs at the annual Spring Special Olympics "Go Fishing" event. (Courtesy of Energen Collection.)

In association with the Energen Leadership Association, employees spent the day helping the Birmingham and Jefferson County special needs children bait and catch fish at the Oak Mountain State Park. (Courtesy of Energen Collection.)

It was not the size of the fish that counted—it was the amount of fun had by the participants. The pride of team members in their successful "catch of the day" made the day worthwhile. (Courtesy of Energen Collection.)

In January 1999, many Alagasco employees volunteered their time to help renovate the Head Start Fairmont Center for pre-school children. (Courtesy of Energen Collection.)

Employees also landscaped with shrubbery and bark. (Courtesy of Energen Collection.)

(*left*) Alagasco purchased new playground equipment and painted the exterior and interior of the center. (Courtesy of Energen Collection.)

(*right*) Andre' Taylor, vice president of communications, spent the day painting at the center. (Courtesy of Energen Collection.)

Alabama Gas traces its support of Junior Achievement back to 1954, when chairman of the board Howard Higgins started the first Junior Achievement program in the state while he was serving as Opelika district manager. (Courtesy of Bud Hunter.)

Jim Rutland (left) and Betty Griffin (standing, second from the right) help a couple of Junior Achievers work on salt-and-pepper shakers for Han/d Products. Alabama Gas sponsored the Jefferson County Junior Achievement class. The group formed the Han/d Products Company that made and sold auto trouble lights and salt-and-pepper shakers. Alabama Gas employees volunteer their time to serve as advisors. (Courtesy of Energen Collection.)

A five-member team from Montgomery's commercial office competed in the Third Annual American Business Women's Association "Strut" (fast walk). The money raised went to charity. (Courtesy of Energen Collection.)

The BEAT Project was a way for Energen employees to help someone who is willing to help him or herself. BEAT had a goal to build about 60 new homes in the Ensley/Sandy Bottom section of Birmingham as part of a neighborhood revitalization effort. BEAT used volunteer labor to help build a home for someone who is willing to get involved by investing his or her own seat equity in the project. Energen had more than 100 employees that gave up one or more Saturdays to come out and get splinters and aching backs. Everyone got involved—even the chairman of the board. (Courtesy of Billy Brown.)

Energen employees support the American Red Cross in a variety of ways, but the most well known are the semi-annual blood drives. The coordinators of the blood drives have been quite inventive over the years to increase the number of participants using the lure of T-shirts or drawings for a prize such as a trip. Others used the approach of competition between collegiate pride rivals Alabama and Auburn to get loyal fans to give blood in honor of their team. (Courtesy of Energen Collection.)

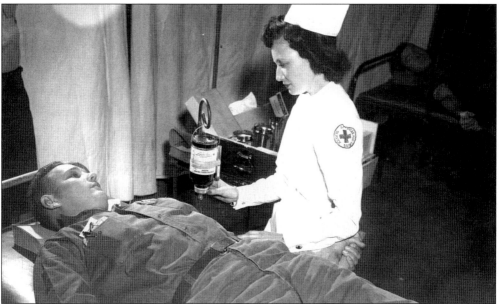

Many company employees have been the keys to saving a human life by giving a priceless possession—blood. The influence of Alagasco's first president, Joseph Greene, continues into the 21st century as Energen continues to have Red Cross blood drives twice a year. Greene, as chairman of the Birmingham Red Cross, was responsible for the decision to add Red Cross to the United Appeal (later known as United Way). (Courtesy of Energen Collection.)

Alagasco president Mike Warren met President Reagan, June 18, 1986 in the White House Rose Garden to accept an award bearing the Presidential Seal. The award was the nation's highest honor under Reagan's Private Sector Initiatives Program. Alabama Gas was the only company in Alabama and one of only two utilities in the President's Award for Private Sector Initiatives. (Courtesy of Energen Collection.)

Operation Assist instilled a sense of pride and confidence in its workers. For many participants that originally entered the program searching for summer income, it became more than just a job. (Courtesy of Energen Collection.)

Operation Assist ran for seven years and was a way for the company to help low-income customers by weatherizing their homes. It also gave the company employees an opportunity to get involved in helping the customers. In addition, the company hired low-income youths to do the work. It was a win/win situation for everyone involved. (Courtesy of Energen Collection.)

You want to see an employee with a new attitude about customer service? Let him or her go out and work on a customer's home that has holes in the roof where the rain comes in. They never look at customers quite the same again. They become very interested in the welfare of the people they work for, because they see them as people—not just numbers. The program ended in 1991 after Energen/Alagasco had weatherized more than 50,000 homes. (Courtesy of Energen Collection.)

One of the students employed in the Operation Assist program, Terry Smiley, came to work for the company upon his graduation from college. Terry is the third from the left on the back row in this group picture. He worked as an installer in Talladega in 1988 and 1989 for the Talladega Division. (Courtesy of Energen Collection.)

In 2000, Terry Smiley became district manager of Jasper. Smiley stated that Operation Assist taught him "to always do the best I possibly can, and do the job right."

Preparing Christmas shipment to Vietnam are, from left to right, John Salter (assistant supervisor-data processing), John Lathram (highway coordinator-technical services), and Leonard Grefseng (supervisor-printing department) all members of Alagasco's Birmingham District Supervisors Association. The group sent five cases of candy, a television antenna, a length of television cable, and plastic tablecloths for Christmas to the men of Battery "B" 2 Battalion, 33 Artillery, Army First Infantry. Earlier in the year, the Association sent a short wave radio and items for the local orphanage. (Courtesy of Energen Collection.)

Alagasco donated 15 two-way radios to Civil Defense Corps in April 1961 to be used in the Birmingham area. Alagasco continued to contribute to the Civil Defense Corps—in 1963, the company gave 35 mobile radios. A Civil Defense spokesperson stated that this would provide Civil Defense part of the necessary equipment required to inform the public should the need arise. (Courtesy of Charlie Preston Studios.)

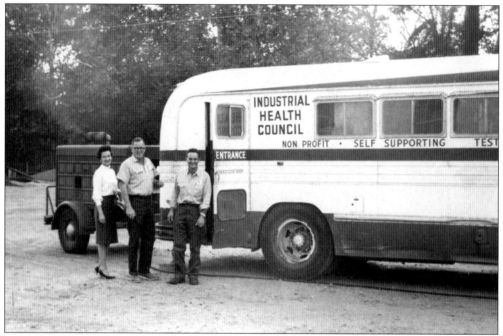

Alagasco joined forces with the Industrial Health Council in its first year of operation. The Council was composed of several hundred industries and business firms in the Birmingham area. The objective was to make chest x-rays available free of charge to all employees and members of their families. These tests were done in the mobile x-ray unit in June 1948 and continued for many years. (Courtesy of Energen Collection.)

The purpose of the chest x-ray was to find tuberculosis in the early, curable stage. The results of the test were confidential and only the individual concerned given the result of the test. The Industrial Health Council and Alagasco collaborated for a number of years to encourage good health for employees. (Courtesy of Energen Collection.)

In October 1986, the restoration of the old depot began with the objective to provide new office space. The revitalization of an old train station, the Seaboard Railway Station, made good use of property for Alabama Gas and the city. This was another way that the corporation demonstrated its commitment to support downtown areas. (Courtesy of Energen Collection.)

Once the restoration was completed, Alabama Gas located its Birmingham commercial office and a portion of its customer call center in this building. (Courtesy of Energen Collection.)

In July, 2000, *GASLINES* reported that 43 new CNG buses were coming to the streets of Birmingham to help combat the city's air quality problem and its persistent "non-attainment area" status. The Environmental Protection Agency classifies a "non-attainment area" as an area where air pollution levels are often unhealthy. First Transit, the company that replaced Birmingham's Metro Area Express, formerly known as MAX, was the only public transportation authority in the state that uses CNG technology in its bus fleet. (Courtesy of Energen Collection.)

The desire for alternative fuel usage includes the introduction of CNG use in Alagasco vehicles. Here, local students learn about the environment and alternate fuels such as CNG. (Courtesy of Billy Brown.)

(*above, left*) Energen employees inspect an area for environmental issues and concerns before the expansion of a pipeline into the area. (Courtesy of Billy Brown.)

(*above, right*) Water testing regarding environment is just one of the ways that Energen and its subsidiaries adhere to EPA regulations. (Courtesy of Billy Brown.)

The boat, dubbed the *MERV-1* (short for Methane Energy Research Vessel), made its maiden voyage as the first shrimp boat to be powered by LNG, or liquefied natural gas, in 1987. (Courtesy of Energen Collection.)

In 1966, the company changed the color and look of the automotive fleet. A two-tone blue paint job replaced the old black and gray decorative theme. A new sign appeared on the doors of the vehicles. The sign was made reflective so that it stood out in brilliant yellow. In addition, the traditional yellow striping on the rear of all trucks was also in reflective tape, a move toward safety on the road at night when the vehicles so often were out providing that service. (Courtesy of Graphic Photo Service.)

TIMELINE—CHARITIES

1844 YMCA started in England.
1851 YMCA started in United States.
1858 YWCA started.
1878 Salvation Army started in England.
1879 Salvation Army started in United States.
1881 American Red Cross.
1887 Charities Organization started in Denver, Colorado (United Way).
1910 Camp Fire USA.
1911 Children's Hospital.
1913 American Society for the Control of Cancer (American Cancer Society).
1924 American Heart Association.
1940 Catholic Family Services.
1949 United Cerebral Palsy.
1971 Sickle Cell Disease Association of America.

Energen has been working with charities and providing for the less fortunate in the communities of Central Alabama since 1948. The following is a sample of charities and programs that have been helped by Energen.

American Red Cross
United Way
Adopt-A-School
Arthritis Foundation
Alabama Symphony
American Heart Association
American Cancer Society
Bread and Roses
Boy and Girl Scouts
BEAT Project
Cahaba River Society
Christmas in April
Crisis Center
Gatekeeper
Goodwill Industries
Junior Achievement
March of Dimes
Salvation Army
Workshops, Inc.
Operation Assist (Recognized by President Ronald Reagan)

Four

THE GLOW OF
THE FLAME

The customers and stockholders are the glow of Energen's flame. Without their partnership and satisfaction, the flame would not grow brighter. Throughout the company's history, this partnership theme has continued, especially relating to customer relations. Alagasco's marketing programs changed from Old Stove Roundups to "Real People, Real Choices," yet the intended audience remained consistent—current and potential customers. The corporation's approach included developing partnerships, listening to the customers, and the personal touch on difficult conversions. Energen's aggressive growth strategy implemented in fiscal year 1996 focused on enhancing shareholder value. In 2000, the completion of an exciting five-year period demonstrated sustainable, long-term earnings growth for its stockholders. Total shareholder returns were 230 percent over the 5-year period, for an annual compound growth rate of 27 percent.

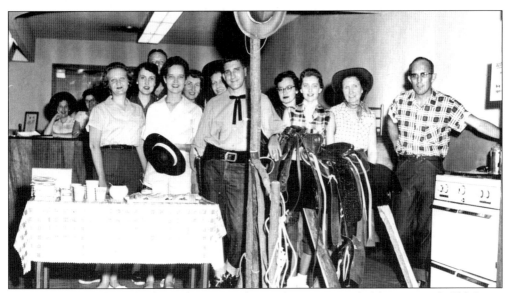

From the 1940s through the early 1960s, the marketing group held an annual Old Stove roundup. This competition between the different locations was an effort to increase sales and market share. The winning location received a trophy to be kept at the local "ranch" until the next competition. (Courtesy of Energen Collection.)

When Birmingham Gas and Illuminating Co. received its franchise in 1879, the city included a special notation. The proposed 20 street lamps were to operate on a "moonlight schedule" and used only on nights when there was no general illumination from the moon's light, as was "customary in other cities." Today, streetlights can be illuminated even on a full moon. (Courtesy of Billy Brown.)

Mike Warren, chairman, president, and CEO-Energen, was featured on the cover of the December 2001/January 2002 issue of *American Gas* magazine. The article, "Powerful Partnerships," documented Warren's history with Energen and outlines his goals for his term as chairman of American Gas Association. (Courtesy of Billy Brown.)

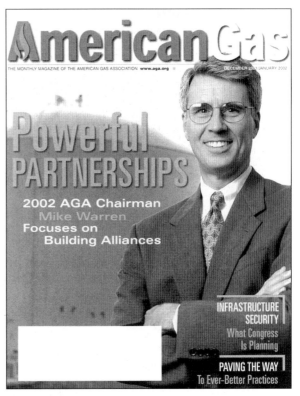

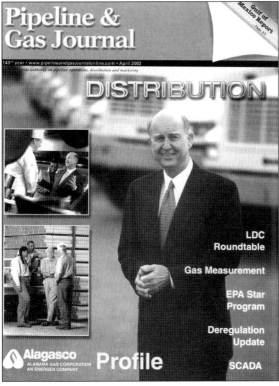

Gary Youngblood, president of Alagasco, was featured on the April 2002 cover of *Pipeline and Gas Journal*. The article "Alagasco's Marketing Strategy: Remember Who Pays the Bills," profiled Youngblood's management style for dealing with customers and employees. (Courtesy of Geoff Knight.)

Gaslights remained a part of the products sold and serviced by Alabama Gas Co. In 2001, Montgomery employees converted two antique gaslights from electricity. The lights, marked "made in Birmingham, England 1810," were originally powered by gas and then, according to the homeowner, converted to electric power in the 1970s. The lights were so large that Mike Bailey, service mechanic, had to custom-build open flame burners. Other Montgomery employees involved in the conversion were Craig Carter, Roosevelt Ware, Mike Jarman, Ed McCall, Dwain Young, and James Thompson. (Courtesy of Energen Collection.)

Over the years, customers identified the gas company with different employees of the company. For example, in the 1800s and early 1900s, the lamplighters were seen on a routine basis, as they would light the lamps in the evening and put them out in the mornings. Lamplighter W. Frank Gray, installation and service department, is shown lighting a gas street lamp at the Birmingham Service Center in October 1958. (Courtesy of Energen Collection.)

Alagasco Lamplighters in the lamp division serviced and cleaned the lamps after installation. In 1852, Mr. Foster, a resident of Holcombe Street, lit the lamps in the evening and extinguished them in the morning. He was paid $35 per month. It is reported that he rode a big gray horse and stood in the saddle to reach the lamps. (Courtesy of Energen Collection.)

In 1966, a group of four Alagasco employees from the Birmingham District used their ingenuity to market gas lights. W.C. Bracknell and three other installation and service mechanics equipped his truck with gaslights, grills, and bottled gas. Each of the men scheduled time to travel the area and sell gaslights and grills from the back of the truck. The men were Ray Lee, A.L. Abney, W.C. Bracknell, and W.W. Wyatt. (Courtesy of Graphic Photo Service.)

In February 1955, Liberty National Life Insurance Co. asked Alabama Gas to provide the flaming torch for the 38-foot replica of the Statue of Liberty that adorns their home office. The flame was to appear to be burning oil. For this visual effect, it was necessary that it be quite yellow. A very yellow flame is unstable and easily extinguished by even moderate winds. However, the problem was attacked with much interest. Using tin cans and baling wire for experimental materials, a burner producing a flame that was pleasing to both Alabama Gas and Liberty National resulted. On September 13, 1958, the Liberty National's statue was lit. Throughout the statue's history, Alagasco answered the call to keep the torch lit. Most recently, the natural gas torch at Liberty Park was repaired in March 2001. Officials at Liberty Park called Alagasco after receiving numerous telephone calls from motorists asking why the torch was out. The torch was cleaned and a faulty component replaced. Now the torch burns each day between 3 p.m. and 2 a.m. and Miss Liberty continues lighting the way to freedom with a natural gas torch. (Courtesy of Energen Collection.)

As street lamps changed designs and no longer required daily lighting, meter readers became the more recognizable employees. Meter readers and repairmen used various types of transportation, including motorcycles, to cover their assigned routes. Cal Russell, pictured here in 1949, had worked for Alabama Gas and its predecessors for 33 years in Tuscaloosa. When Cal started in 1916, his first mode of transportation was a wagon and Ol' Dan. (Courtesy of Energen Collection.)

This is a meter from 1900 used to measure manufactured gas. The company finished converting from manufactured gas to a natural gas system in 1954. (Courtesy of Universal Photo Service.)

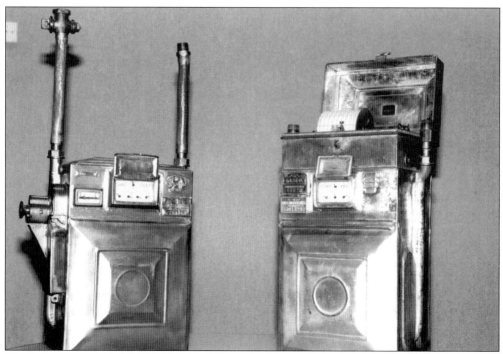

There were various types of meters produced over the years. One type of meter required tokens or nickels that allowed gas to flow into the residence. (Courtesy of Energen Collection.)

In 1949, Alagasco sold Servel Air Conditioners as another way to increase the number of customers using gas. Selma employees sold an entire carload of Servel All Year Gas Air Conditioners. (Courtesy of Energen Collection.)

Alagasco salesmen and employees participated in the annual "Stove Roundup." They encouraged current customers to trade in their old stove for a modern gas stove. Each "ranch location" wanted to win the competition. The locations would have square dances or parades with salesmen on horseback to promote the roundup. (Courtesy of Energen Collection.)

In addition to the employees dressing in cowboy and cowgirl attire, advertising on the delivery trucks was another way to promote the Old Stove Roundup each year. (Courtesy of A.C. Keily Studio.)

In April 1964, gas advertising began "traveling" Alabama highways for first time. Painted on the side of the company's huge trailer truck is an eye-catching illustration and the words, "Heat and Cool with year-round gas air conditioning," which would be seen throughout Central Alabama. Alagasco's trailer van logs between 1,800 and 2, 000 miles per month traveling on a regular schedule around the company's service area redistributing all types of gas appliances arriving in Birmingham via rail and truck. Proudly displaying this first "traveling billboard" is Charles H. Lama, general superintendent of the Birmingham district. Driving is Ray C. Trousdale of the Storeroom Department. (Courtesy of Graphic Photo Service.)

Marketing representatives held parades and other events to encourage customers to trade in their older stove for a new gas stove as part of the annual Old Stove Round-Up. (Courtesy of Energen Collection.)

The concept of partnerships has been a part of the Energen philosophy for many years. In addition to using traveling billboards on cars and trucks, the company used traditional billboards like this one to remind people that Alagasco was interested in developing partners with various resellers and sellers. This sign was located at the entrance road for the Pinson LNG plant in 1965. (Courtesy of Energen Collection.)

Alabama Gas Corporation used its logo of a young Native American with a blue flame as his feather for several years. The character's name was "Alagasco." Many of the marketing items and company vehicles and products included an image of him. Alagasco changed logos in 1978 to reflect a new look that company officials wanted to convene the message that this was a company of today and tomorrow. (Courtesy of Energen Collection.)

Using a new technique for marketing, sales personnel set one-night records. Weeklong campaigns increased sales of gaslights and gas grills in several districts. Alagasco and Southern Natural Gas joined teams in this new technique. The formula was simple. Southern Natural sent one of its colorful carousel trucks into neighborhoods along with Alagasco sales, office, and service personnel where they would ring doorbells, show off equipment, and close sales. The carousels, pennants flying, had four different types of gaslights mounted on a platform on the trucks and two others, with full-length posts, stationed at the rear. Bottled gas provided the fuel to keep the lights burning throughout each tour. (Courtesy of Graphic Photo Service.)

Marketing representatives used a float with both gaslights and gas grills in parades through downtown Birmingham. During the parade, employees grilled hamburgers and handed them out along the parade route. (Courtesy of Graphic Photo Service.)

Mrs. Frank E. Prady is shown above being interviewed by Dave Overton of the radio station WBRC, while Mrs. Elyse Van Dyke and Miss Virginia Tullis serve the buffet luncheon in June 1948. In the background is Archie Barr, who sold the "CP" Magic Chef range to Mrs. Prady. WBRC carried these radio broadcasts each Tuesday and Thursday in 1948. The program, "At Home with Mrs. Birmingham," continued with increasing enthusiasm on the part of homemakers. From 18 shows recorded in 11 different communities, 267 housewives heard the "Gas Has Got It" story and enjoyed the food prepared using the CP range. Some part of every menu came from the Silent Servel refrigerator. (Courtesy of Almon Photo Company.)

After the purchase of an IBM 1401 computer system, the company completely converted the customer billing and accounting. The result was the design and implementation of a one-sided gas bill with advertisements on the reverse side. (Courtesy of Energen Collection.)

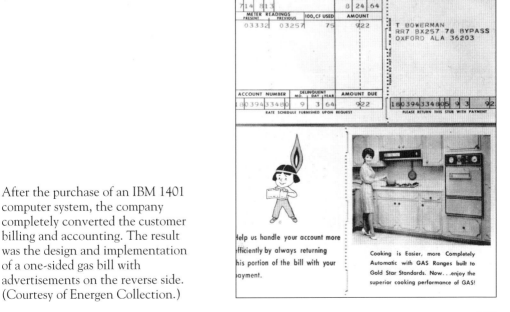

To promote the selling efforts of gaslights in 1966, a large gaslight display greeted all visitors as they entered the Birmingham headquarters. (Courtesy of Graphic Photo Service.)

Desiring to increase the number of customers using gas or number of gas appliances per household, the company developed a marketing promotion using retail stores. In addition to a show area at EGN, Alagasco opened gaslight and grill stores in the Birmingham district. The stores promoted a variety of energy-efficient natural gas products, such as fireplace logs, grills, and gaslights. (Courtesy of Billy Brown.)

This picture from 1955 shows Howard College home economic students practicing modern gas cooking on one of the two kitchen units equipped with appliances on loan through Alagasco's school program. (Courtesy of Charlie Preston Studios.)

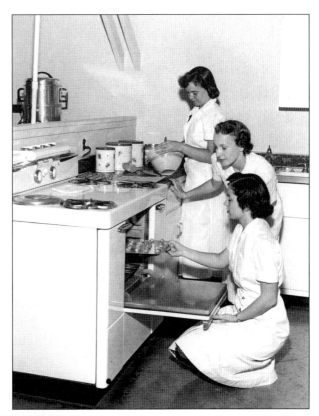

The "good old days" were the days when gas was largely manufactured instead of natural, and appliances were quite crude and inefficient by today's standards. The convenience and speed of automatic gas cooking, refrigeration, central heating and cooling, and thermostatic controls were either unknown or available only to the wealthy. (Courtesy of Albert Kraus.)

WVTM Channel 13's "Top O' The Morning" show spawned a cookbook with Chef Clayton Sherrod on the front cover. It benefited the United Way Food Bank in 1991 and 1992. Cooks throughout the state purchased the right to share a few culinary secrets with Alabama's top chefs, while allowing Alagasco an opportunity to help feed Alabama's hungry by raising over $9,000. (Courtesy of Energen Collection.)

When customers purchased a new stove, the company provided a cookbook that introduced them to natural gas cooking techniques. (Courtesy of Energen Collection.)

On October 18, 1948, this group handled more than 2,800 calls from customers during one day—more than four calls a minute. Through these telephones flow more than 100,000 calls for service every year. Pictured from left to right are Mildred Carter, Mary Thompson, Dee Winger, Gloria Flack, Bertha Lee Davis, Jessie Westbrook, and Byrda Ennis. Seated on the table at the left is Sid Gunter, who was in charge of the operation. The wheel in the center of the table held current calls waiting to be handled by servicemen in the field. (Courtesy of Energen Collection.)

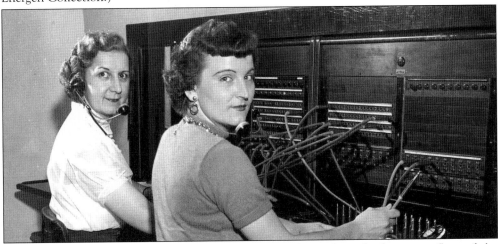

Shown at work in the switchboard room, which was located on the basement floor of the Birmingham offices, are Bernice Baker (left) and Ida Webb. These operators exemplified "the voice with the smile." Their pleasant, courteous manner makes thousands of friends for Alabama Gas and means dollars and cents to business. Knowing that customers will judge the company largely by helpfulness of employees' telephone attitudes, these operators think of the telephone as a doorway to Alabama Gas. Theirs is a key position in the communications system. In handling literally thousands of calls annually, they put out the "welcome mat" as courtesy to customers is traditional with Alabama Gas employees. (Courtesy of Kealen Rice.)

Anne Powers conducted a customer service training program to enhance the service that the customers receive. This was part of company-wide customer service training incentive to re-energize Alagasco's customer care efforts. The two-day training session was entitled "Achieving Extraordinary Customer Relations." (Courtesy of Billy Brown.)

Employees play a vital role in increasing the number of Alagasco customers. The company devised incentive programs to reward employees that bring in new "tips" over the years. In 2000, Sharon Ray, a customer service representative in Tuscaloosa, won a trip to the destination of her choice for selling five tips. (Courtesy of Energen Collection.)

In 1955, the employee sales tip campaign was a success. Cash winners in the group drawer at the Birmingham main office included Helen Cowan, Emily Loyd, Ann Jones, Ann Weldon, Clifton Burnham, Helen Kieran, and Mary Jo Garrett. (Courtesy of Charlie Preston Studios.)

The Pride Celebration for 1989 commemorated reaching the 400,000-customer mark at Fair Park Arena. It was the culmination event of Customer Appreciation Days. After two weeks of letting customers know how much Alagasco appreciated them, the Pride Celebration showed Alagasco employees how much their work was appreciated. (Courtesy of Energen Collection.)

During the celebration, Larry Neeley, chief operating officer of the American Meter Company, presented Alagasco with a gold meter. A huge, 807-pound cake spanned three tables and formed the number 400,000.

Alagasco installed its 10,000th meter in the Selma community on November 7, 1967, and celebrated the milestone by honoring the homeowners where the installation was made with a gold meter, a gaslight, and a gas grill. Sgt. Charlie Jones of the Selma police department and Mrs. Jones were the fortunate customers at whose home the unusual meter was placed. Attending the ceremony were Selma District Manger Joe D. Patrick; Chamber of Commerce President Edgar Russell; Mayor Joe Smitherman; Sgt. and Mrs. Jones; S.F. Wikstrom (Alagasco's vice president of marketing); and Selma District Sales Manager Ray Parnell. (Courtesy of Energen Collection.)

In March of 1999, the Selma Division converted 120 apartments from electric heat and water heat to natural gas. Some of the Selma employees involved with the meter installation at the Cloverdale Apartments included Ray Hardin, Johnny Harris, Darrell Bruner, Robert Nichols, James Moore, Phillip Howell, Thomas Ferguson, and Jerry Chance. (Courtesy of Energen Collection.)

In 1993, Mercedes announced plans to build its first American car plant in Vance, Alabama. The plant uses natural gas as one of its energy sources. (Courtesy of Energen Collection.)

When its newly constructed radial tire plant was at full production capacity, Goodyear in Gadsden had the world's largest tire facility. Built alongside an older Goodyear plant making conventional tires since 1929, the new radial tire plant opened in March 1978. Over the years, Alagasco categorized Goodyear as a large industrial customer in the Gadsden area. (Courtesy of Energen Collection.)

Alabama's Livestock Coliseum, the dream of the Alabama Agricultural Center Board, was completed in 1954. The building, which was the largest state-owned enclosed arena in the world for its time, also had one of the largest and most modern exclusively gas-fired heating systems in the area. Natural gas was also used in the emergency lighting system. When a power system failure occurred, a natural gas driven generator system had the lights back in operation within six seconds. (Courtesy of Horace Perry.)

Alagasco Service Centers are important plant facilities to keep close to the customer base in each location. Montgomery service centers have changed over the years to improve service and the working environment of the employees. This photograph shows one of the earlier centers in Montgomery. (Courtesy of Stanley Paulger.)

With Elmore County identified as the third fastest growing county in 2002, the Montgomery Service Center continues to play a vital role in providing services to the local customer base. (Courtesy of Energen Collection.)

In 2002, Alagasco trucks are equipped with tools and supplies that employees may need at a construction site or on a service call.

ALAGASCO TOTALS

	TOTAL OPERATING REVENUE	TOTAL TAXES PAID	TOTAL MILES OF MAIN	TOTAL NUMBER OF CUSTOMERS
1940	$4,367,000	$77,000	340	20,640
1950	$11,008,000	$611,000	1,497	133,900
1960	$33,647,000	$1,756,000	3,135	220,000
1970	$58,280,000	$2,830,000	4,816	307,000
1980	$260,822,000	$14,681,000	6,027	351,000
1990	$309,304,000	$19,896,000	7,509	400,500
2000	$399,900,000	$30,200,000	10,710	465,700

Five

THE FLAME
GROWS BRIGHTER

One hundred and fifty years ago, the vision was to light the streets of Montgomery, Alabama. Within two years of the vision, the first gas streetlights were lit for the state capitol city. The vision grew from there. And today, just as Miss Liberty's natural gas torch flame continues to glow brightly in Birmingham, so does the future for Energen and its customers and shareholders. For Energen and its employees, their torch flame is a statement of principles: "We will conduct our business and earn a profit based on ethical standards and values which recognize the dignity and worth of all individuals, commitment to excellence in performance, personal and business integrity, and courage of convictions and action."

In 2002, Energen and its subsidiaries celebrate 150 years of business operations. One might think that after a century and one-half of existence it is time for to rest and watch the sunset. Yet, for this corporation and its subsidiaries, this celebration means it is time to look to the future and plan for the next century and beyond. It is a time to anticipate the new challenges and opportunities within the energy industry. (Courtesy of Energen Collection.)

One hundred and fifty years ago, the vision was to light the streets of Montgomery, Alabama. Within two years of the vision, the first gas streetlights were lit for the state capitol city. The vision grew from there. And, today, just as Miss Liberty's natural gas torch flame continues to glow brightly in Birmingham, so does the future for Energen and its customers and shareholders. (Courtesy of Energen Collection.)

Epilogue
IT'S ALL ABOUT
THE PEOPLE

Energen's history is rich with individuals who contributed to its longevity and success. Members of the past and present board of directors provided guidance through the years. Past and present officers developed programs and initiatives for continued growth and success. Employees, both past and present, worked to meet each challenge and opportunity.

It's all about the people . . .
(Courtesy of Billy Brown.)

124

125

127